From Mealworm to Beetle

Following the Life Cycle

by Laura Purdie Salas
illustrated by Jeff Yesh

PICTURE WINDOW BOOKS
Minneapolis, Minnesota

Thanks to our advisers for their expertise:

Celeste Welty, Ph.D.
Extension Entomologist & Associate Professor of Entomology
Ohio State University

Terry Flaherty, Ph.D., Professor of English
Minnesota State University, Mankato

Editor: Shelly Lyons
Designers: Nathan Gassman and Lori Bye
Page Production: Melissa Kes
Associate Managing Editor: Christianne Jones
The illustrations in this book were created digitally.

Photo Credits: Newtilus/istockphoto, 23.

Picture Window Books
151 Good Counsel Drive
P.O. Box 669
Mankato, MN 56002-0669
877-845-8392
www.picturewindowbooks.com

Printed in the United States of America.

 All books published by Picture Window Books
are manufactured with paper containing at least
10 percent post-consumer waste.

Library of Congress Cataloging-in-Publication Data
Salas, Laura Purdie.
From mealworm to beetle : following the life cycle / by Laura Purdie Salas ;
illustrated by Jeff Yesh.
p. cm. — (Amazing science: life cycle) Includes index.
ISBN 978-1-4048-4925-9 (library binding)
1. Meal worms—Life cycles—Juvenile literature. I. Yesh, Jeff, 1971- ill. II. Title.
QL596.T2S25 2009
595.76—dc22   2008006435

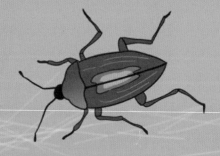

Table of Contents

Big Change

A darkling beetle begins life as a mealworm. But it will change forms and grow up to be an adult beetle. There are many kinds of beetles. Let's look at the life cycle of the darkling beetle.

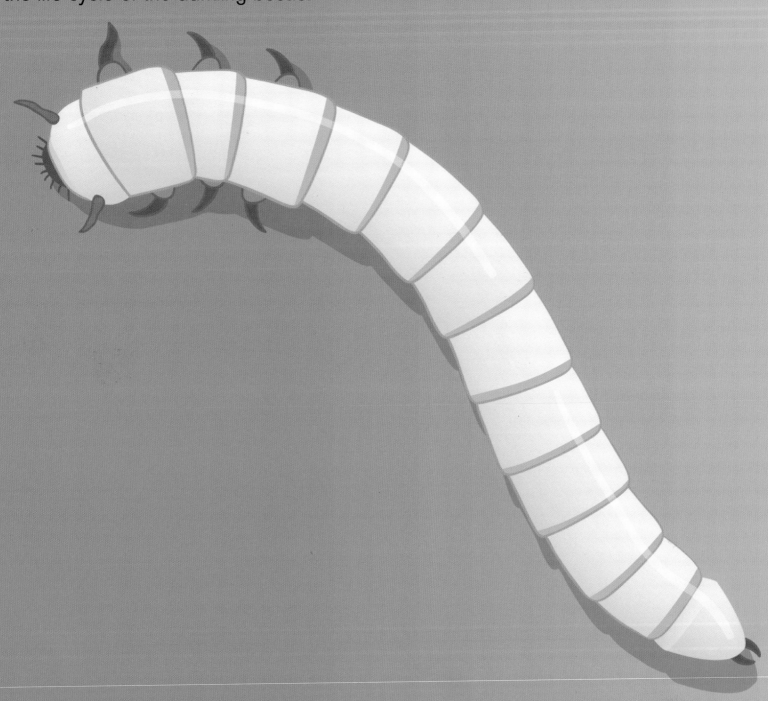

Many children study the life cycle of darkling beetles in the classroom. The animals are small and simple to take care of.

A Beetle's Beginnings

The darkling beetle's eggs are shiny white ovals. The adult female beetle lays her eggs near grain or in barns. Grain will be the mealworms' food. Four to 19 days will go by before the mealworms hatch from the eggs.

A darkling beetle's egg is about the same size as a pinhead.

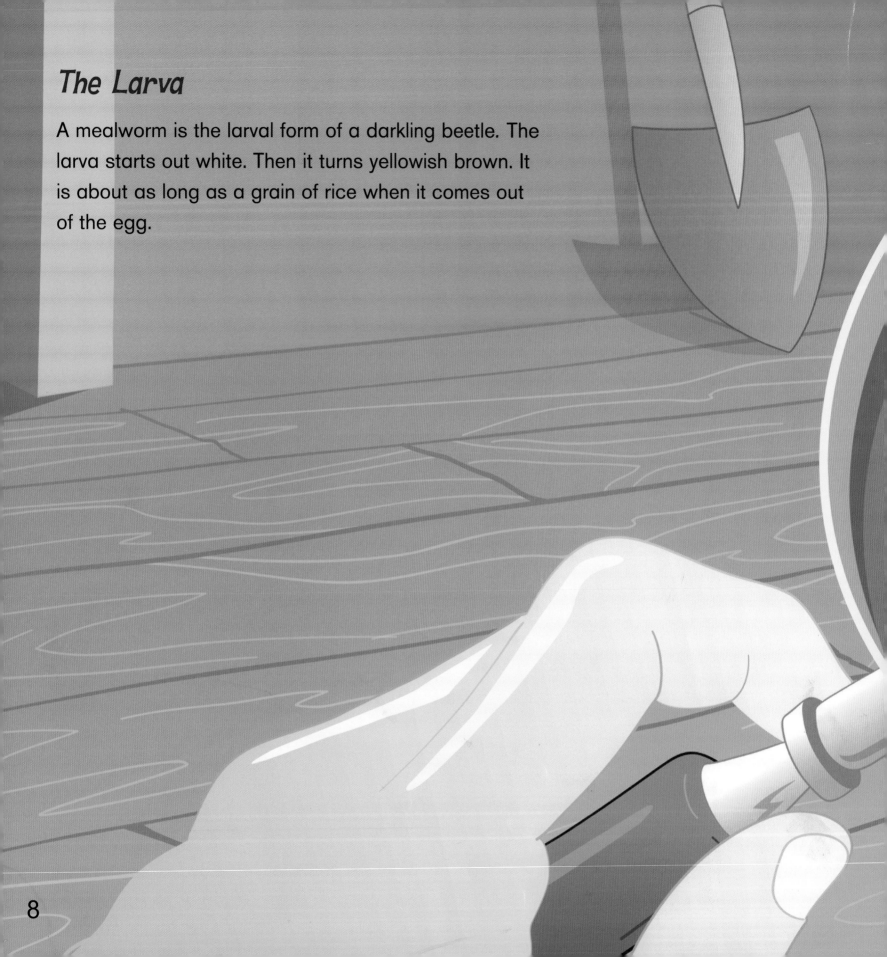

The Larva

A mealworm is the larval form of a darkling beetle. The larva starts out white. Then it turns yellowish brown. It is about as long as a grain of rice when it comes out of the egg.

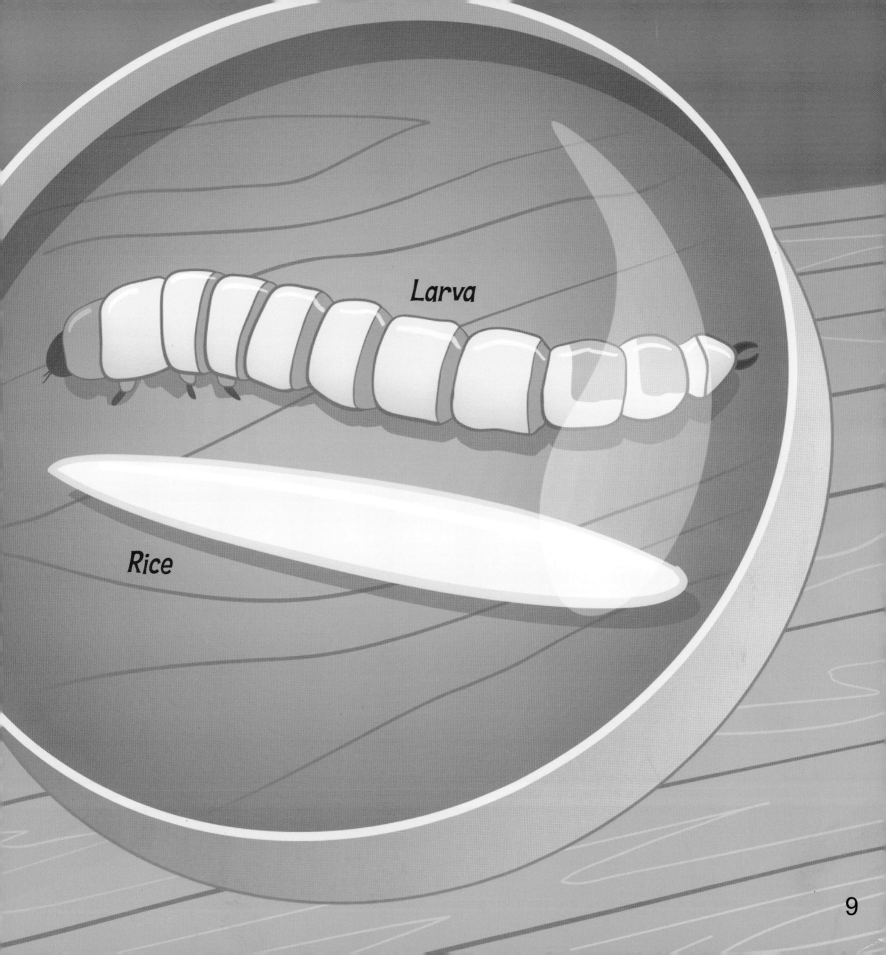

When Is a Worm Not a Worm?

The mealworm looks like a worm, but it is an insect. It has a shell called an exoskeleton. The shell is made up of many plates. This shell protects the mealworm's insides.

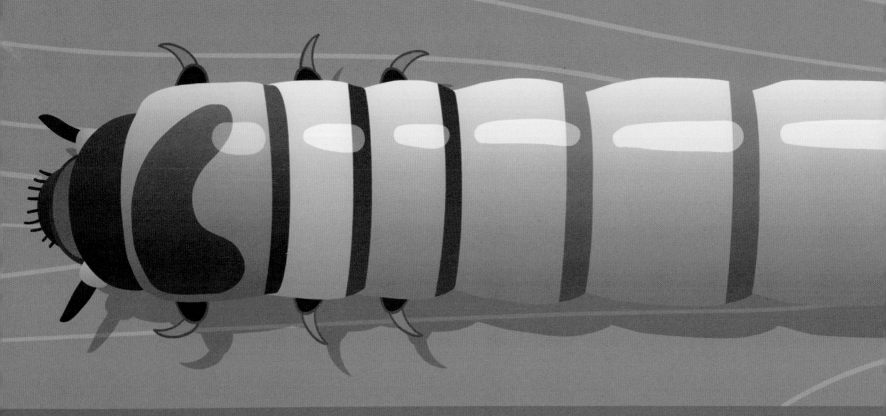

The mealworm has six stubby legs. They are all
crowded around the front of its body.

Shedding the Shell

When the mealworm gets too big, its exoskeleton splits open. The soft larva crawls out of the shell. This process is called molting. Once the new exoskeleton hardens, the larva will eat and grow. A mealworm molts 14 to 15 times over many months.

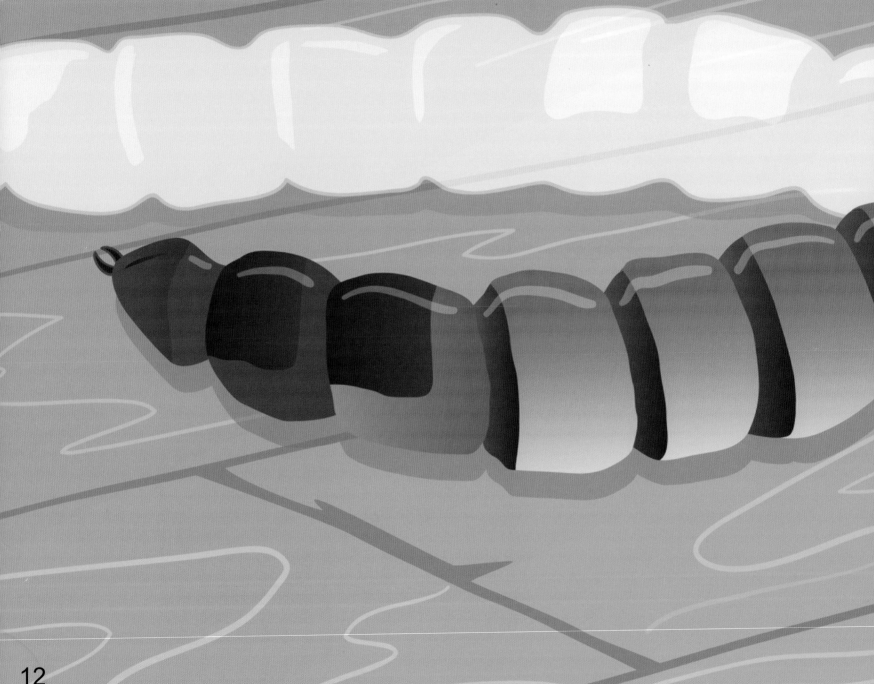

The larval stage usually lasts from six to nine months. But it can last as long as two years. If the environment is cool, the larva will take longer to develop.

A Case for Change

The final time a mealworm sheds its shell, it turns into a pupa. The pupa is a bit longer than a staple. It is white and feels like leather. It has a head and a pointed tail.

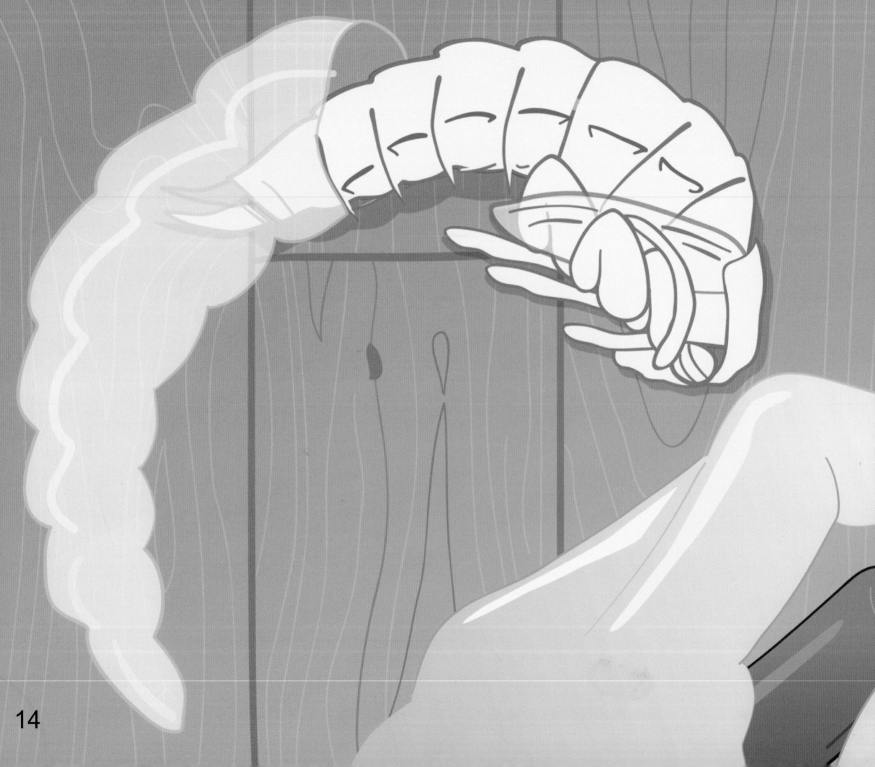

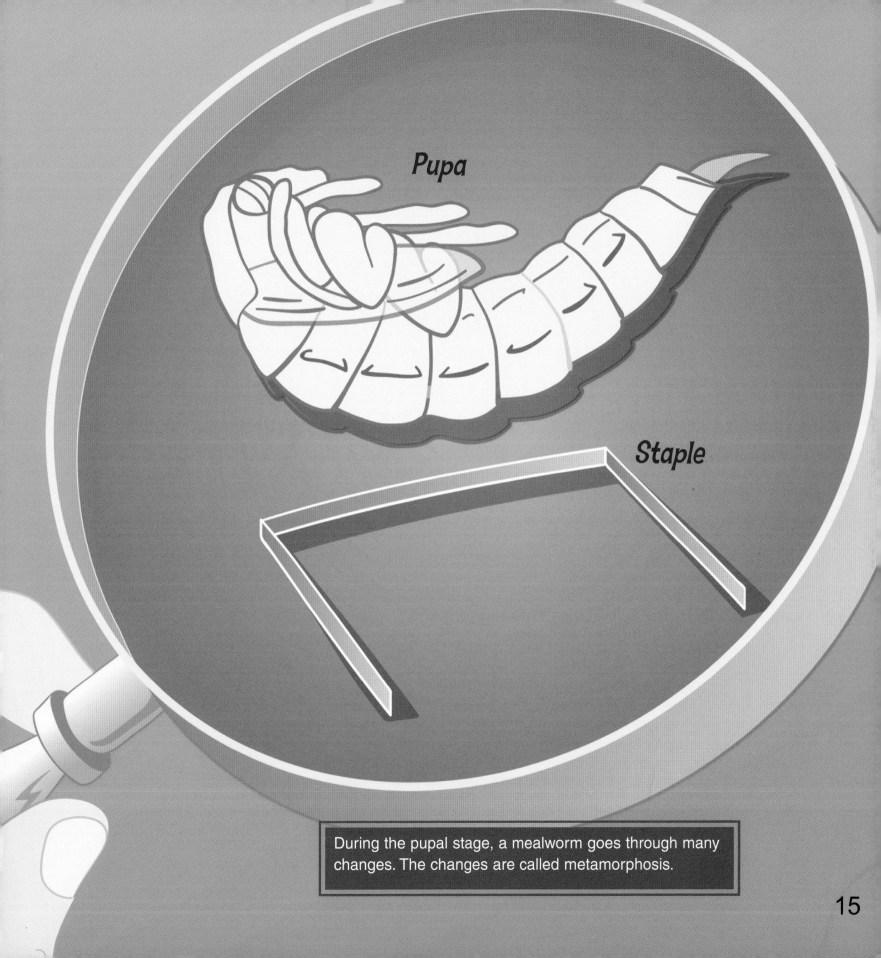

Pupa

Staple

During the pupal stage, a mealworm goes through many changes. The changes are called metamorphosis.

15

The Life of a Pupa

Inside the pupa, the mealworm breaks down its body. It then forms adult body parts, such as the legs, antennae, and wings. The pupal stage usually lasts about two weeks.

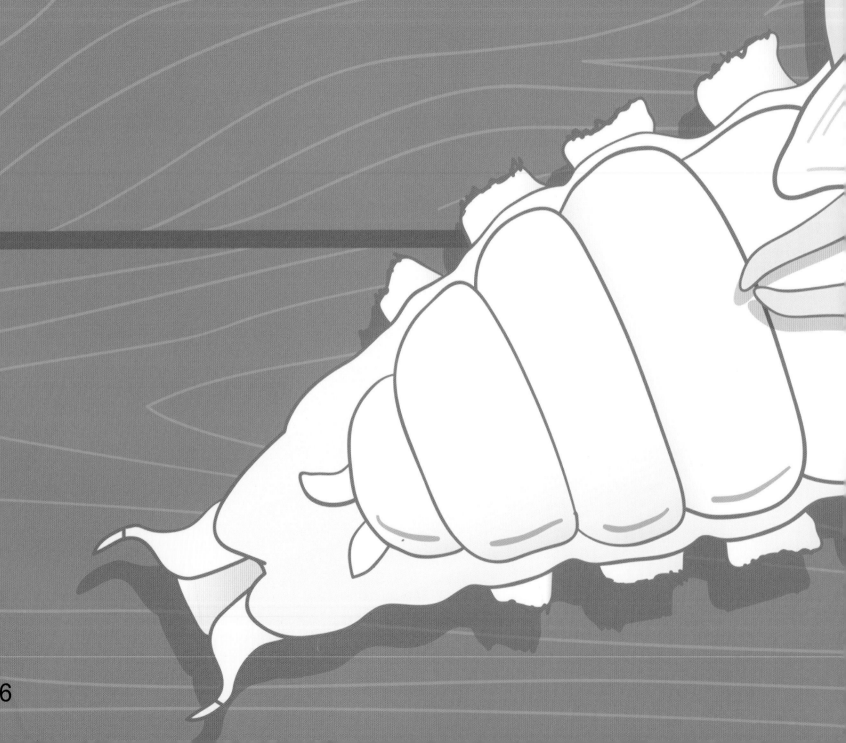

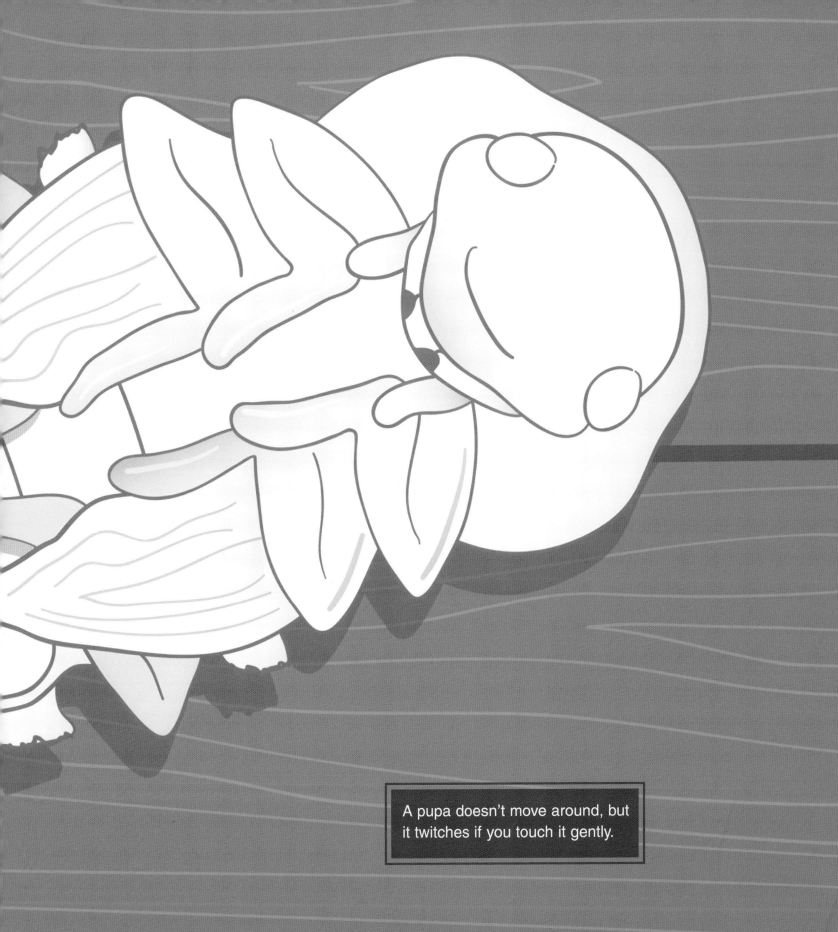

A pupa doesn't move around, but it twitches if you touch it gently.

Finally, a Beetle!

At the right time, the exoskeleton of the pupa cracks and splits open. An adult darkling beetle crawls out. It is white at first, but it quickly turns black.

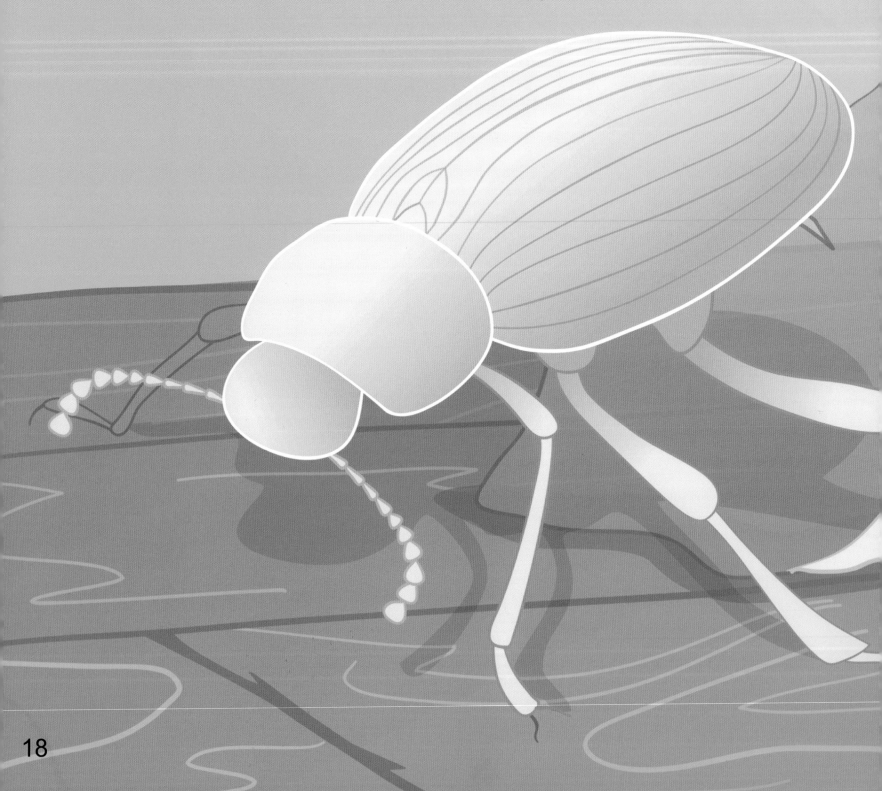

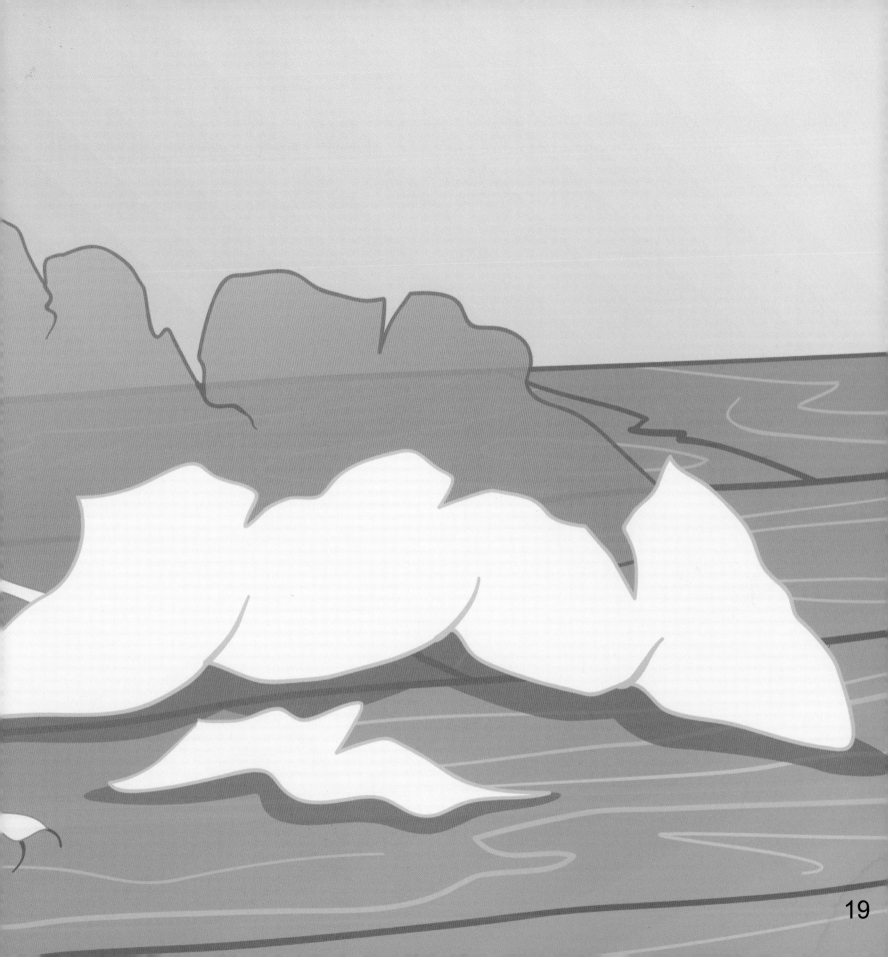

Mating

Adult beetles find mates. After mating, the female beetles lay as many as 1,000 eggs. They lay the eggs where there is plenty of food. The mealworms that will hatch from the eggs will eat this food.

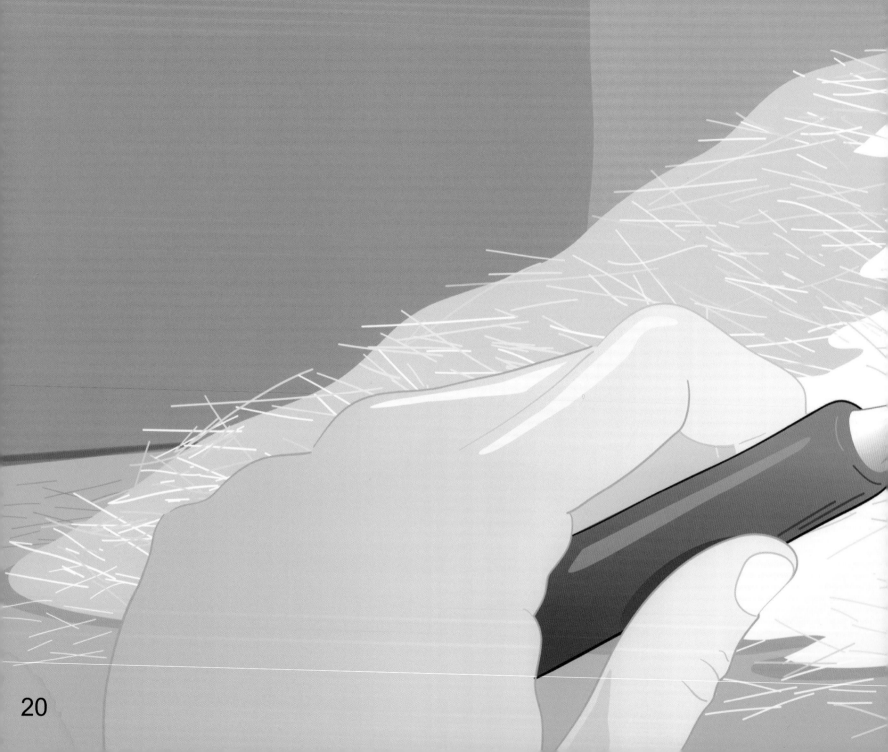

Darkling beetles have a short life cycle. They usually live for about one year.

Life Cycle of a Darkling Beetle

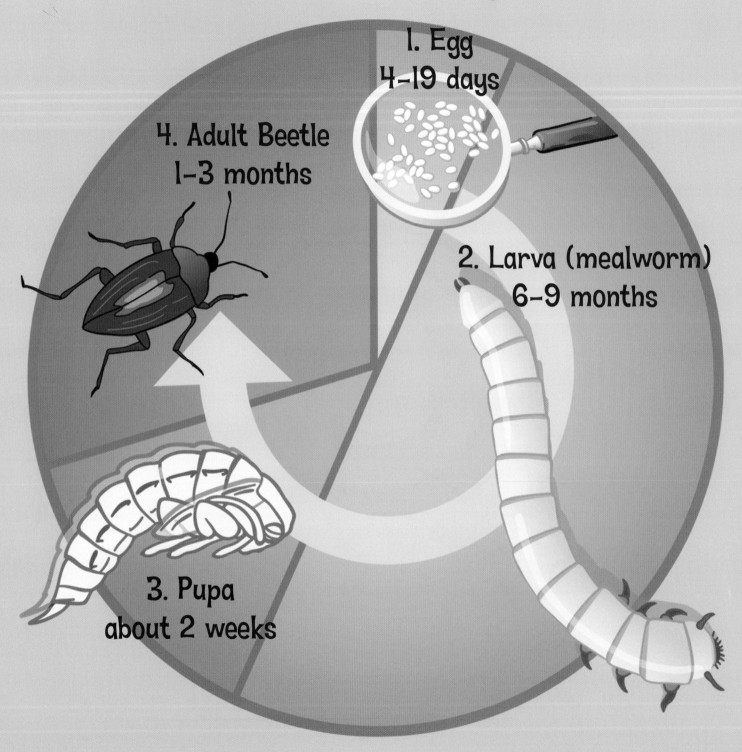

1. Egg
4-19 days

4. Adult Beetle
1-3 months

2. Larva (mealworm)
6-9 months

3. Pupa
about 2 weeks

Fun Facts

- Mealworms and darkling beetles live all over the world, except in Antarctica and the Arctic Circle.

- Mealworms have simple eyes that can tell light from dark. They prefer darkness.

- While mealworms shed their skin 14 to 15 times, most insect larvae shed their skin only three to four times.

- The life cycle of a mealworm happens much faster in a classroom because the food, light, and temperature can be controlled.

- Mealworms are named after the food they eat—grain, or meal.

Mealworm

Glossary

antennae—feelers on an insect's head used to sense and touch; more than one antenna

exoskeleton—a shell or covering that protects an animal's soft body

grain—the seed of grasses such as wheat or barley

larva—the stage after an insect egg hatches

mating—joining together to produce young

metamorphosis—changing from one form into a very different form, like a caterpillar to a butterfly

molting—shedding fur, feathers, or an outer layer of skin; after molting, a new covering grows

plates—large, flat, usually tough structures on the body

pupa—a hard casing with an animal inside; the animal is changing from larval stage to the final animal stage

To Learn More

More Books to Read

Himmelman, John. *A Mealworm's Life.* New York: Children's Press, 2001.

Kalman, Bobbie. *Animal Life Cycles: Growing and Changing.* New York: Crabtree Pub. Co., 2006.

Schaffer, Donna. *Mealworms.* Mankato, Minn.: Bridgestone Books, 1999.

On the Web

FactHound offers a safe, fun way to find Web sites related to topics in this book.

All of the sites on FactHound have been researched by our staff.

1. Visit www.facthound.com
2. Type in this special code: 1404849254
3. Click on the FETCH IT button.

Your trusty FactHound will fetch the best sites for you!

Look for all of the books in the *Amazing Science: Life Cycles* series:

From Caterpillar to Butterfly: Following the Life Cycle

From Mealworm to Beetle: Following the Life Cycle

From Puppy to Dog: Following the Life Cycle

From Seed to Daisy: Following the Life Cycle

From Seed to Maple Tree: Following the Life Cycle

From Tadpole to Frog: Following the Life Cycle